# The Essential Guide to Horseback Riding For Parents of New Riders

By
MARY KAY DELGADO

*The jargon, etiquette, acronyms and other enigmas of the sport explained so you can stop looking dazed and start having fun at the barn.*

A Mole's Mountain Book
published by Dos Madres Press Inc.
P.O.Box 294, Loveland OH 45140

ACKNOWLEDGEMENTS

*Thank you to the trainers, parents, and students who have pa-
tiently answered my questions during lessons and shows. I am
especially grateful to Gretchen for sharing her time and technical
expertise. Thanks to Sr. Helen Jean for her editing prowess, and
to my focus group, Chile, Barb, Mary Beth, Joy, Gina, and Jeff.
Thank you to Katy, Kelly and John for their insight into retail. And
thank you to Maddie, who pulled me into the barn and encour-
aged me to learn.*

Book Design by Elizabeth Murphy
www.IllusionStudios.net

ISBN 978-1-933675-39-8

*This book is dedicated to those parents who are not naturally drawn to horses, but enter the barn anyway, to better understand their child's passion.*

# Prologue

When my daughter turned five she announced that she wanted a pony. Instead I got her a book about horses.

When she turned six she asked for horseback riding lessons. Instead I took her to ride ponies at the fairgrounds.

At seven, she repeated the request for horseback riding lessons. But I was fearful of horses and knew nothing about the sport. In my mind, her unwavering fascination with horses called for more advanced distraction techniques. Over the next four years I enrolled my daughter in ballet and piano lessons. She tried cheerleading, volleyball and track. By age 11 she was asking for horseback riding lessons again, and this time she was not to be dissuaded.

I cringe remembering that my primary criterion for the classes was that the barn be close to home. I was oblivious to the risks, unaware of the different riding styles, and couldn't tell the difference between a well-run barn and one that was mediocre. It's a miracle that my daughter received the good foundation that she did.

This simple guide is written for those of you who find yourselves in the same situation. If your horseback riding experience consists solely of a guided trail ride while on vacation, this little book will give you the basics you need to:

- Find a reputable place to ride
- Purchase the proper attire
- Understand competitions
- Keep your child safe

This is a practical guide written by a parent for other parents new to the sport. It does not pretend to be a thorough technical manual written by an equestrian expert. However, the information provided in this guide has been reviewed by experienced trainers to ensure its accuracy.

– Mary Kay Delgado

# Table Of Contents

# 1. Learning To Ride

So your daughter wants to ride! For her, horseback riding lessons will be a dream come true. She will not even realize that she is learning responsibility, patience, and the rewards of hard work. You will know she's growing in confidence though, when that slip of a girl is able to control an 800 pound animal.

Before choosing a place to ride, you need to know what riding style your daughter is interested in learning. That choice is an important first step because the riding style will determine the kind of training pursued, the horses used, and the type of clothing and equipment needed.

## RIDING STYLES

There are two widely recognized riding styles from which to choose, namely, Western and English. Lessons in either style will teach a student the basics of how to ride a horse. There are subtle differences in how a rider holds the reins and sits in the saddle when riding English compared to Western and the horses are trained to recognize different commands. What really distinguishes one style from the other is the type of competitive events they each hold.

### WESTERN

Western competitions can include:

▶ Trail classes in which riders guide their horses through a course simulating the obstacles encountered on a trail ride.

▶ "Reining" which showcases the riders' ability to lead their horses through complicated patterns with spins and turns.

▶ Halter classes in which a horse is led in their halter by their rider.

▶ Contests that include timed barrel racing and pole bending (weaving in and out of a row of poles as quickly as possible).

When competing, riders wear western style shirts with sequins and embroidery and their boots are of the cowboy variety. A western saddle has a saddle horn in front and show saddles can be very fancy with silver embellishments. If you would like to see Western riding in action, you might catch a demonstration at the local county fair.

**ENGLISH**

There are three main types of English-style competitions:

### ❯ *Hunter/Jumper*

This is the most popular form of English riding and it is considered an Olympic sport. Riders jump fences of different heights according to their level of ability. Hunter competitions are judged on the skill of the horse, while jumper competitions are timed. School age riders commonly jump fences up to three feet in height while professionals can jump five feet or even six feet high. Riders wear special shirts with a removable collar, tailored jackets, special breeches, gloves, and tall leather boots.

### ❯ *Dressage*

Dressage is also practiced at the Olympics. The best way to describe dressage is that the rider directs the horse in precise, special movements without any visible signals. For example, the rider may ask the horse to walk in place, take elongated strides, or walk sideways. It takes an experienced rider and a trained horse to compete in dressage. Riders wear fancy jackets with tails, high collared shirts, gloves, and top hats.

### ❯ *Cross Country*

This form of horseback riding can be the most dangerous and requires an enormous amount of skill, analogous to extreme skiing. Riders and their horses jump a number of obstacles over the length of a course covering several acres of field or woods. It requires tremendous endurance and speed. There is no special dress other than safety gear. At the lower level, cross country competitions may be held locally as stand-alone events and are referred to as "hunter trials." More commonly, it is one of the components of "Eventing".

## ❯ *Eventing*

Experienced riders compete in three-day events encompassing dressage, cross country, and stadium jumping. Each portion of the competition is scored by giving penalty points for errors committed. The horse and rider with the lowest combined score over the three days wins. In dressage, a penalty might involve the horse taking an incorrect number of steps during a required movement. Penalties arise in cross country and stadium jumping when a horse refuses to go over a fence, knocks down fence rails, or fails to finish within the allotted time period.

The remainder of this guide focuses on the English Hunter/Jumper style of riding and the basic information you need to know as the parent of a new rider.

# 2. Where To Take Lessons

There are three kinds of barns to consider for lessons. As you research your options, keep in mind that you are looking for a "trainer" and not a teacher.

## PRIVATE FARMS WITH THEIR OWN HORSES

If you know someone who owns a horse, they might be willing to give your daughter lessons. The advantage is that they would presumably charge less than a trainer and it would be an inexpensive way for your daughter to learn the basics of riding. However, if she becomes serious about competing or joining a riding team, you will need a trainer with the appropriate level of experience and teaching ability. It can be difficult, expensive, and time consuming to un-do poor riding habits.

## BARNS THAT BOARD HORSES FOR OTHERS

Stables sometimes have boarders or grooms who are willing to give classes. Again, this might be an economical solution for a beginner but a serious student needs proper training which you may or may not find. Also, using a boarder's horse for classes can be a complicated affair. (For more on this topic, see the section on "Leasing").

## TEACHING BARNS

A teaching barn will not be your cheapest alternative, but it has many advantages. First, there are several ways to judge the reputation of the barn. The easiest is to visit your local tack store, a store that carries everything needed to ride or to take care of a horse. The employees at the store will know all of the local barns and trainers and may be willing to provide some insight into their teaching style.  The other way to judge the quality of the trainers is to attend a local horse show and observe how the trainers interact with their students. Any barn or tack store will be able to tell you when and where the next shows are to be held.

A teaching barn will have dedicated trainers who will emphasize safety. They will also focus on the riding skills needed to compete and guide you through the show process. Another plus is that this kind of facility will have "school horses," horses purchased specifically for use by students in lessons. This saves you the challenge of dealing with a horse's owner. Since there are multiple horses to choose from, it ensures that your daughter is riding a horse that is matched to her ability. In addition, a teaching barn will provide everything a rider needs to mount a school horse, such as a bridle, halter, and saddle.

Barns, like trainers, have distinct personalities. Some are very competitive and are best suited for the serious riding student who will take multiple lessons per week and travel out of state for shows. Others may be technically competent, but focus on the fun of riding which is more appropriate for a younger rider or a recreational competitor. You will want to visit two or three before making your final decision.

# 3. Lesson Logistics

In most cases, you will be expected to sign a liability waiver before taking lessons. A rider can get kicked or fall off of a horse and both circumstances can result in injury. However, if you have a good trainer and your daughter follows directions, you will have considerably less risk. Every rider falls off of her horse at some point, and usually she is able to brush off the dust and get right back on.

Because there is always a chance that your rider could get hurt, you, or another adult you trust, need to stay for your daughter's lesson. Besides being present in case of emergency, watching the class and helping tack up the horse are the best ways to learn about the sport.

## BEFORE EACH LESSON

During your daughter's first lessons, she will learn how to get the horse ready for riding. It will not take long for her to master the steps, and then she will be expected to prepare the horse on her own and be ready to ride when the lesson starts.

Plan to arrive a half hour early in order to get the horse ready for the lesson. There are several steps to follow:

1. Put the horse's halter on and attach the cross ties.
2. Brush the horse all over to get the dirt off its coat.
3. Pick dirt out of the horse's hoofs.
4. Put on the saddle pad, saddle, and girth.
5. Adjust the length of the stirrups.
6. Take off the halter and put on the bridle and bit.
7. During fly season, apply fly spray.
8. Double check that the girth fits snugly.

## AFTER THE LESSON

Plan to stay at the barn for a half hour after the lesson while your daughter lets the horse cool down, untacks the horse, cleans the tack, hoses down the horse, and gives it a treat. You may want to set a clear time limit and have your daughter wear a watch; otherwise she may proceed to visit every other horse in the stable and give them treats as well.

## FEEDING

Every horse receives a different combination of hay, grain, and water based on its size, age, and level of activity. Most barns mark the animal's diet on a board outside its stall. Bales of hay come apart in squares called flakes and horses receive a certain number of flakes each day.

Typically riders are not responsible for feeding the horses as it can cause confusion about which animals have been fed and when. Leave the feeding to someone knowledgeable about the horse's diet. However, if the trainer approves, you may give a horse a piece of apple or a carrot as a treat.

To give a treat, open your hand with your palm up. Place the treat on your palm and let the horse take it with its lips. If you are worried about germs or slobber, carry wet wipes in your pocket. Never offer a treat with your fingers as the horse will try to grab it with its teeth and may accidentally bite your fingers.

Horses love peppermints, too, but again, ask the trainer's permission first and be careful to throw away the candy wrapper so that the horse does not eat it.

## MUCKING STALLS

If your daughter is taking lessons at a barn, chances are she will not have to clean out the stall. However, she does need to learn how it is done and cleaning the stall is part of the bonding process between horse and rider. Once your daughter feels comfortable around horses, she might offer to muck stalls in exchange for lessons or riding time.

# 4. Clothing and Equipment

| CLOTHING/ EQUIPMENT | BEGINNER | COMPETITIVE |
|---|---|---|
| **Helmet** | An equestrian helmet looks like a bike helmet but it is made differently to protect against a very different type of fall. Riding helmets must be "ASTM/SEI" approved for safety. Some barns have spare helmets they are willing to lend for a beginner's first class, but then you need to buy the real thing. Have your rider's first helmet fitted by a knowledgeable salesperson. $40-$120 | Traditionally show helmets were covered in velvet, but now velveteen and suede are acceptable. Helmets with a vent down the front are particularly popular. Beware: a riders' hair has to fit completely under the helmet, so make sure there is enough room when she tries it on. There is a difference between helmets used for dressage versus hunter/jumper competitions. $100-$500 |
| **Paddock Boots** | You can get away with a closed toe boot with a heel in a pinch, but you really want a sturdy boot that can withstand wet conditions and a horse stepping on the rider's foot. Invest in a pair of paddock boots specifi-cally designed for working and riding. They provide extra support in the ankle that a rider needs. Pad-dock boots come in lace up and zip up styles. Leather zip-up boots are the more popular of the two but the lace-up style is best for extra narrow or wide feet. Synthetic boots are available at the lower end of the price range. $40-$180 | Only young riders can wear paddock boots instead of tall boots. Your trainer will know which is appropriate. |

| CLOTHING/ EQUIPMENT | BEGINNER | COMPETITIVE |
|---|---|---|
| **Paddock Boot Socks** | Okay, no one will be able to see the socks the rider is wearing, so anything goes. However, the socks made for paddock boots are cushy and just the right height and weight to keep the boot from rubbing against the ankle. Plus they don't slide around on the foot. $5-$10 | Only appropriate for young riders (see above). |
| **Riding Gloves** | Riding gloves come in many styles and colors. They help the rider grip the reins and protect their hands from getting hurt. Regular knitted winter gloves won't work. $10-$60 | A must for showing. Black is always appropriate. |
| **Half Chaps** | Chaps are worn with paddock boots and cover the calves to protect pants from rubbing against the horse. The chaps/ paddock boot combo with jeans is the everyday alternative to breeches and tall boots. $35-$180 | Not applicable. |
| **Jodhpurs** | Pants specifically designed for young riders with an elastic band at the hem that goes around the boot to keep the pants from riding up. They come in many colors and designs for lessons. | These pants are worn by young riders with paddock boots and garters instead of tall boots. Only beige or khaki pants are appropriate for shows. Check with your trainer as to whether jodhpurs would be appropriate in your daughter's division. $50-$200 |

| CLOTHING/ EQUIPMENT | BEGINNER | COMPETITIVE |
|---|---|---|
| **Belt** | Not necessary. | A must. Any kind will do but brown is the all around safe choice. |
| **Tall Boots** | Be thankful that they are not necessary for every-day lessons. | A must for competitions unless the rider is ten or under in which case she will use jodhpurs and paddock boots instead. Tall boots come in two styles, either the kind you pull on with a special tool called a boot pull or the kind that zip up the back. Boots that zip up are easier to get on but the zippers tend to break after a couple of years as the leather wears. Boots are further differentiated between those with laces, called a field boot, and those without, called a dress boot. Dress boots are required for high level dressage. Tall boots need to be fitted by someone in the know to make sure they are the correct size for the foot and calf, as well as the correct height. Do not attempt this on your own! It is difficult to find tall boots on con-signment. Expect to pay between $160-$380 for leather boots. Synthetic boots are now available for less than $100 as is a rubber version that may be acceptable at certain shows. |

| CLOTHING/ EQUIPMENT | BEGINNER | COMPETITIVE |
|---|---|---|
| **Boot Bag** | Not necessary. | The boots are expensive and need to be in pristine condition for shows, so riders put them on just before the competition and take them off right after. To protect them you will want to get a boot bag. It is difficult to find a substitute that is big enough or protects the finish properly. (Let's face it, pulling the boots out of a pillow case just looks tacky.) You can find a nice boot bag for as little as $25. |
| **Boot Socks** | Not necessary. | Here again any kind of sock will work because the judge will not be able to see them. However, boot socks are made the proper length and weight for tall boots. They are also slippery and help the boots slide on. Although the judge will not see the socks, the riders will because they take off their tall boots when they are not in the ring. So the socks have become a fashion statement among the competitors and are available in many designs and colors. $8-20 |

| CLOTHING/ EQUIPMENT | BEGINNER | COMPETITIVE |
|---|---|---|
| **Riding pants/ Breeches** | Jeans or other long pants will do for classes but the raised inseam can rub the inside of the knee and leave a sore spot. Form fitting riding pants are more comfortable. Get a professional's opinion about the fit before you buy. $40-$120. | Fitted riding pants in beige or khaki are a must. Tailored Sportsman is a well known brand often used to describe the classic pant style. There are many new brands that look like the Tailored Sportsman. A slightly looser style is the rage right now. $40-$250. |
| **Garters** | Not necessary. | Leather straps worn just under the knee with jodhpurs. These are only necessary if your daughter is not wearing tall boots. Plan on asking for help to put them on properly the first time as they do not come with instructions and it is not obvious. $29 |
| **Shirt** | T-shirt or other form fitting shirt. | Polo shirts may be worn at informal barn shows or for jumper competitions. However, all other shows require that girls wear a long-or short-sleeved collarless oxford shirt with a removable band around the neck. A regular col-lared shirt is not accept-able for girls. Boys wear an oxford shirt with a tie. $40-$150 |
| **Hairnet** | Some trainers require hairnets during lessons while others do not. | A must at shows unless your rider is ten or under in which case you can get away with pig tails and bows. $2 for three. |

| CLOTHING/ EQUIPMENT | BEGINNER | COMPETITIVE |
|---|---|---|
| **Show Jacket** | Not necessary. | Beginners competing in a fun show might be able to get away with a boy's navy blue suit jacket ($10 at a resale shop). However, show jackets are form fitting and the cut is noticeably different. Young riders grow so quickly you are better off borrowing a jacket or buying one second hand until you know they are serious about the sport. $120-$450 |
| **Rubber Boots** | Good to have if you are going to be mucking stalls, but not appropriate for riding. These have become another fashion statement and come in many designs and colors. $30-$100 | Not applicable. |
| **Tack trunk** | Not necessary. | If your daughter becomes a serious competitor or you buy your own horse, your trainer may request that you purchase a certain kind of trunk so that all of the competitors from the barn have the same style. $600 and up. |

**Please note:**

Beware!  Your daughter will also want:

A garment bag for her show jacket that will match the boot bag.

A bag for horse supplies and the supplies themselves.

A bracelet with her favorite horse's name inscribed on it.

A horse.

# 5. Horseback Riding Jargon

For those of us who have never ridden horses before, the barn can be a mysterious place. To begin with, it has its own special vocabulary. Below is a review of the jargon commonly heard around the barn. This list will save you from having to ask, "What does that mean?" over and over again to the annoyance of the barn staff, students, and other parents.

## ❯ GETTING THE THREE "E'S" STRAIGHT

**Equine:** Anything having to do with horses.

**Equestrian:** Anything having to do with horseback riding.

**Equitation:** The ability of a rider, as in, "She has good equitation." This involves sitting in the proper position on the horse as well as making the horse move properly.

## ❯ PEOPLE AND PLACES

**Trainer:** Horseback riding teacher. Using the term "teacher" immediately identifies you as a novice.

**Barn:** To the uninitiated, a barn is a place for keeping animals and storing farm implements. However, for the horseback riding set, the "barn" refers to the riding establishment, as in, "What barn do you ride at?" or "Mom, can you drive me to the barn?"

**Paddock:** The field where the horse is kept when outside.

**Ring:** Area where the riders practice. The ring can be either indoors or outdoors. You will definitely want to find a barn with an indoor ring if you live anywhere the temperature is likely to drop below 40°.

**Stall:** The specific space assigned to a horse in the stable.

**Stable:** The building housing the stalls.

**Tack store:** A store that carries all of the clothing and paraphernalia needed to ride and care for a horse plus horse-related books, magazines, and gifts.

## ❯ RIDING ATTIRE

**Paddock boots:** Short leather (or pleather) boots worn when working around horses.

**Breeches:** These are stretch pants with patches along the inside of the leg that prevent wear due to rubbing against the saddle.

**Jodhpurs:** Riding pants worn by younger riders with paddock boots instead of tall boots.

**Chaps:** Suede or leather leggings worn over pants for day to day riding in place of the more expensive breeches. Think cowboy attire.

**Half chaps:** Chaps that only cover the rider's calf. These help the rider grip the saddle with her legs when riding.

## ❯ HORSE ATTIRE

**Tack:** All the horse's gear – bridle, bit, reins, saddle.

**Lead rope:** A long rope used like a leash to walk a horse.

**Halter:** The equivalent of a dog collar for a horse, a halter makes it easier to catch, hold onto, or tie up the horse.

**Bridle:** Similar to a halter but with a metal piece, called the bit, that goes into the horse's mouth. The reins are attached to the bit and help the rider steer.

**Saddle pad:** A soft, quilted or fleecy pad that goes on the horse's back under the saddle to protect the skin from rubbing directly against the leather.

**Girth**: A wide band that buckles onto the saddle, goes under the horse's body, and buckles to the saddle on the other side. It keeps the saddle from sliding off the horse.

**Martingale:** A strip of leather that runs from the bridle under the horse's head to the girth under the horse's body. It keeps the horse from being able to raise its head beyond a certain level.

**Crooper:** Paraphernalia for the back end of the horse. The crooper is a leather strap that attaches to the back of the saddle at one end and goes around the horse's tail at the other. It can help keep the saddle in place on smaller animals.

## ❯ OTHER HORSE-RELATED JARGON

**Cross ties:** In a horse's stall, or in a common area used for grooming the horses, there are typically two long ropes hanging against opposite walls. When the horse needs to stand still for grooming, one rope is attached to each side of the horse's halter to keep it from walking away.

**Groom:** The person who brushes the horse before and after it is ridden, and tacks up for the rider. If you are not careful, this could easily become your job.

**Crop:** A short whip held by the rider and used occasionally to encourage a slow or disobedient animal.

**Hoof pick:** A metal tool used to get dirt out of the bottom of the horse's hoof.

**Lame:** Any number of ailments causing a horse to limp or favor one leg over another (and one of several reasons why you might not want to buy a horse). Typically a lame horse cannot be ridden.

**Pulling the mane:** This is not as painful as it sounds and is actually a way to trim the horse's mane in preparation for a show.

**Farrier** or **blacksmith:** The person who specializes in shoeing the horses.

**School horse:** A horse used by the barn offering lessons.

**Lessons:** Instruction at the barn.

**Classes:** Competitive events at a show.

**Schooling the horse:** The practice of riding the horse prior to a show to reinforce the signals and commands it should know.

**Pony:** Contrary to popular, misinformed belief, a pony is not a baby horse. It is a type of horse that never grows as large as a regular horse. Ponies are referred to as small, medium, and large.

**Hands:** A way to measure the height of a horse, a hand is the equivalent of four inches. By definition, a pony is never taller than 14.2 hands. A really big horse would be 17 hands.

**Lunge line:** A very, very long leash used in exercising and training a horse.

**Lunge the horse:** The trainer stands in place holding the lunge line while the horse runs in a full circle around her. This is done while training a horse or as a way to have it work off excess energy.

**Cribbing:** When a horse gnaws on the side of its stall. This behavior is obviously detrimental for the stall, but it can also injure the horse's mouth and teeth. A horse may wear a special "cribbing collar" around its neck to help it break the cribbing habit.

## ⟩ RIDING TERMS

**Heels down:** An expression you will hear the trainer repeat over and over again during lessons. It means that when a rider's feet are in the stirrups, her heels should be pointing toward the ground. This helps improve balance and keeps the feet from sliding through the stirrups.

**Squeeze:** During a lesson a trainer will repeatedly ask students to "squeeze." This is a reminder that the rider has to squeeze her legs against the horse as tightly as possible to provide control and directions.

**Stride:** Each time the front legs of the horse reach out to take a step.

**Beat:** A step a horse takes when it is trotting or cantering.

**Trot:**  A two beat gait that is faster than a walk but slower than a canter.  Usually a rider has to post while trotting.

**Posting:**  When the rider rises up and down in the saddle to the rhythm of the horse's trot.  This is more comfortable for both the rider and the horse.

**Diagonal:**  When a horse is trotting, the rider should be up, out of the saddle, when the horse's outside leg is extended in front.  When horse and rider are coordinated, they are "on the right diagonal".  Being on the wrong diagonal can cost a rider points in a competition.

**Sit-a-bounce:**  If the rider is on the wrong diagonal, she can stay down in the saddle for a beat to get back in sync with the horse's trot.

**Two point:**  When the rider leans forward toward the horse's neck and lifts her seat off the saddle like a jockey.  This is an exercise that strengthens the rider's legs in preparation for jumping and is sometimes referred to as "jumping position."

**Canter:**  Rhythmic three beat gate faster than both a walk and a trot.

**Gallop:**  Full speed running. Riders do not gallop during lessons. The only time you will see a horse galloping is if it is running free, on a race track, or involved in a cross country competition in which speed is key.

**Lead:**  When a horse is cantering in a circle, its front leg toward the inside of the circle should always take the first step or lead.  When a horse changes its speed, changes direction or lands after a jump it may "be on the wrong lead" and have the wrong leg stepping out first.  This is a major error in competition and the rider must correct it immediately.

**Flying lead change:**  Some horses are able to self-correct and switch legs mid-stride when they realize they are on the wrong lead.  This is very advantageous in a competition.

**Simple lead change:**  If a horse is not able to self-correct its lead, the rider has to slow the horse to a trot for a few steps to give it a chance to change legs and get back on the right lead.

**Eventing:** When a rider competes in jumping, dressage, and cross country all within a single three-day competition.

## ⟪JUMPING TERMS

**Poles:** Railroad ties or poles lying flat on the ground. Riders are taught how to make the horse walk over poles as the first step in learning how to jump.

**Fences:** Jumps set up in a ring. Fences start at eighteen inches and increase in height in six inch increments.

**Standards:** The posts on either side of the fence that hold the poles or boards in place.

**Crossrails:** Two poles are crossed with one end of a pole attached to a post about 18" off the ground and the other end left on the ground forming an "X". When jumping crossrails, the horse is aiming for the middle, or lowest part of the "X".

**Vertical:** A fence made with a pole or flat board between two standards.

**Oxer:** Two verticles placed back to back to form a wider jump. Also called a "spread."

**Bounce:** Two fences set up so close together that a horse goes over one and then immediately over the other. There is not enough space for the horse to take a stride in between them.

**Roll back:** A sharp turn between fences on a jumping course.

## ⟪PARTS OF THE HORSE

**Withers:** A bone that sticks up between the horse's back and its neck marking the place where the front of the saddle pad goes. A horse is also measured from the ground up to the withers.

**Hind quarters:** The back end of the horse.

**Shoulder:** The top of the front legs where you would expect the shoulder to be.

**Outside leg:** The horse's front leg closest to the railing or fence around the ring.

**Inside leg:** The horse's front leg closest to the middle of the ring.

## ◗ HORSE COLORS

**Bay:** Dark brown with a black mane and tail.

**Chestnut:** Auburn red color

**Palomino:** Beige or golden with a cream colored mane

**Dunn:** Beige with a brown strip down the back

**Grey:** A knowledgeable horse person would never describe a horse as "white." They argue that every horse, unless it is albino, has some grey in its coat or on its nose. So the color "grey" is used to describe everything from what appears to be white to a steel grey color.

**Black:** Again, a horse is rarely described as "black." To qualify as black, the horse must be completely black with black skin.

**Appaloosa:** Looks like it has a spotted blanket over some part of its body.

**Dappled:** Any color with very faint spots.

**Paint:** Any color horse, but typically brown, with big blotches of white all over.

**Socks:** Short white patches just above the hooves

**Stockings**: Tall white patches that extend from the hoof to the knee

**Bald face:** A white face on a horse of a different color.

**Star:** A white mark on the horse's forehead.

**Stripe:** A white stripe down the length of the horse's nose.

**Snip:** A white spot on a horse's nose.

# 6. Horseback Riding Etiquette

**Rule #1:  Don't scare the horses.**

Horses are easily frightened by loud noises and sudden movements.  When scared or "spooked", a horse may buck and throw its rider.  I knew a woman who was thrown from her horse when someone nearby opened an umbrella.  You will want to drive slowly near the barn and refrain from honking your horn near the horses.  If it is windy, take precautions with blowing garbage which can spook the horses.  Do not yell, run, or use a flash until you get a feel for the horses.

**Rule #2:  If you see a horse fly, kill it.**

A horse fly bite is very painful for both humans and horses alike.  It may cause a horse to buck and throw its rider, so kill the flies whenever you can.

**Rule #3:  Watch your feet.**

A horse weighs between 800 and 2,000 pounds so you do not want one to step on your foot.  Always wear closed toe shoes around the barn.  If you are stepped on, do not try to pull your foot away.  Lean into the horse's shoulder until it shifts its weight off your foot.

**Rule #4:  Watch the horse's ears**.

If the horse's ears are pinned back against its head, it does not like you and you should move away.  A horse in a good mood has its ears forward.  If they are moving back and forth, the horse is listening to what is going on around it.

**Rule #5:  Watch the horse's eyes.**

A frightened horse will show you the whites of its eyes.  If you see this, move away from the horse.

**Rule #6:  A horse that is pawing the ground is not happy.**

**Rule #7:  A red ribbon on a horse's tail means it kicks.**

**Rule #8:  When your daughter is riding, do not try to talk to her.**

When your daughter is in the ring, whether for a show or a lesson, do not distract her with questions and comments.  It may seem harmless to ask if she needs a jacket or a water bottle, but she needs to remain focused on her horse and her trainer, not you.

**Rule #9:  Apply fly spray from the bottom up.**

Always apply fly spray first to the lower legs working your way up to the stomach, rump and body.  Spraying the horse's head or back first can cause it to spook.  To apply fly spray to the horse's face, spray your hand and then rub it over the horse's head.

**Rule #10:  To walk the horse, stand to its left and grab the lead rope close to the horse's head.**

Hang on, be firm, and do not let on that you are nervous.

**Rule #11:  Dress for the occasion.**

Most riders want an audience so be prepared to stay and watch her ride.  This means you will want to dress appropriately for the barn and the weather.

In the summer, there will be flies; therefore, wear pants to the barn rather than shorts.  Open toe shoes are the sign of a novice.  Bring sun block, sunglasses and a visor.  Keep in mind that everyone and their vehicles will leave the barn covered in a fine layer of dust.

In the winter, many barns are not heated so you will want to dress in layers, wear warm socks and boots, and keep a blanket in the car. Barns that are advertised as heated often only have space heaters so you will want to dress for the cold.  It is rare to find a barn with a heated view- ing room for parents.  By the end of the class there is a good chance your footwear will be covered in mud, so boots are the best choice.

# 7. Equine Enigmas Clarified

**Horses do not automatically kick anything standing behind them.**

Horses kick more people in the movies than in real life. You can actually walk behind a calm horse as long as it knows you are there. You can do this by first talking to the horse and then keeping your hand on its hind quarters (behind) as you walk around it.

**Not all horses wear horseshoes.**

Horseshoes protect the feet but not all horses need them. Some horses' feet are supersensitive to the shoeing process and so they go without shoes. Horses that wear horseshoes have them changed every six weeks by a farrier who comes to the barn.

**The horses you find at the barn cannot be ridden at a gallop for hours on end like they are in the movies.**

Horses are typically ridden for the length of a lesson and then returned to their stalls to rest until the next day. At busy class times, they might be used for two classes in a row.

**Horses that are foaming at the mouth are not sick.**

Horses foam at the mouth when they are working hard. It does not mean that they are sick. Green foam just means that the horse was eating grass or alfalfa before getting its exercise.

**Horses may be shaved so that they do not get too hot.**

A horse grows an extra warm coat for the winter months, especially if it spends a lot of time outdoors. If the horse were to show in a competition with that heavy coat, the horse could overheat. So some owners clip the hair on the underside and legs of the horse to keep it cool. This is called a "trace clip." Another option is for the horse to wear a blanket which keeps it warm enough to discourage the growth of a winter coat.

**Horses may wear fly masks.**

If you have never seen a horse wearing a fly mask, it is a sight to behold. The mask covers part of the face, eyes and ears of the horse and is made of a fine mesh that allows the horse to see and hear while keeping the flies off the skin.

# 8. Leasing A Horse

If your daughter is smitten with the sport, eventually she will want to ride more often on her own outside of classes. Your options at that point are to buy a horse or to lease. Leasing is a wonderful option for those newer to the sport who are not yet ready to own a horse.

A lease allows your daughter to ride someone else's horse during class as well as outside of class time in exchange for a fee. The terms of a lease can vary widely so you will want to have the terms of the lease spelled out in writing.

Typically the lease allows a single person to ride the horse, no siblings or friends are permitted. However, it may be possible to share a lease with another rider, with each rider paying something less than full price. The disadvantage of sharing a lease is that each rider gets half the riding time and must coordinate schedules with the other rider.

The lease may allow for one, two, or three riding times a week. However, if leasing a school horse, you may need to schedule your riding times around lessons. It can be advantageous to lease a horse in the month your rider plans to compete in a show since a lease may result in lower "horse usage" fees at the competition or a discount on lesson fees.

Typical lease terms include:

- The length of the lease, typically arranged month by month.
- The cost.
- Whose saddle and tack will be used.
- How the horse can be ridden, i.e., over jumps or just for flat work.
- Where the horse may be ridden, whether only in the ring or in the ring and the field.
- What supervision is required, e.g., whether or not a trainer's presence is required.
- Whether the animal can be taken off the premises for a trail ride or competition.
- Who is responsible for veterinary care, grooming, and stall cleaning.
- Whether the student's siblings or friends are permitted to ride the horse.

# 9. Competing In Shows

After your daughter has taken lessons for about a year, she may be ready to compete in a horse show. Your trainer will decide when and where your rider can compete, which horse she will ride, and in which division and classes she will compete. The trainer will submit the rider's name for the show, arrange for the horse to be transported to the show, and coach the rider throughout the event.

Shows may be organized by private barns or local, state or national associations. The level of competition and quality of a show is designated by letters A through D. The best and most experienced riders compete in prestigious "AA" shows while beginners might start with a "D" or "C" show just for fun and practice. In Ohio and Kentucky, the primary English riding competitions are held by the Interscholastic Equestrian Association (IEA), Ohio Hunter/Jumper Association (OHJA), Kentucky Hunter Jumper Association (KHJA), and Tri-state Horse Show Association. Shows and competitions are typically held on weekends.

Shows encompass three broad categories: Equitation, Hunter, and Jumper.

❯ Equitation refers to the judging of the rider's form and ability whether walking, trotting, cantering, or jumping.

❯ Hunter classes are judged on the horse's form and ability rather than on the rider.

❯ The jumper category is based on the speed and agility of the horse and rider rather than on form. The objective of the jumpers is to finish the course in the least amount of time without knocking over fences.

## SHOWS

In shows, riders earn points for their individual riding skills and the top two competitors in each division are typically awarded Champion or Reserve Champion titles. Some barns offer a series of shows during the course of the year.  If a rider competes in multiple shows, then any points they earn are accumulated and prizes are awarded to the riders with the most points at the end the season.  Some barn shows include a division for OHJA meaning that points won at that show count toward OHJA awards.

## OHIO HUNTER/JUMPER ASSOCIATION AND KENTUCKY HUNTER/JUMPER ASSOCIATION COMPETITIONS

Riders who are members of OHJA or KHJA earn points for their individual riding skills at shows throughout the year.  Awards are given at the end of the year to the riders in first through eighth place in each division.  The equivalent of a state championship in equitation is called the "Medal Finals" and the ranking of the competitors is based on their performance in a specific equitation class.

## INTERSCHOLASTIC EQUESTRIAN ASSOCIATION COMPETITIONS

Riders involved in IEA compete as a team as well as at an individual level.

### IEA Team Competition

A group of riders, usually from the same barn, form a team with the riders divided among various divisions according to their ability.  The nice thing about the team concept is that there is usually a place for riders of all experience levels.  However, some teams which are very competitive, may require that the riders compete for a spot.

The whole team is subdivided into a middle school team of riders in 6th through 8th grade and a high school team of riders in 9th through 12th grade.  This is important because the two groups compete for separate awards and sometimes compete on different days.

In a team competition, the hosting barn provides all of the horses, and the riders randomly draw the name of the horse that they will ride. This system really tests the skill of the rider since they may not have ridden that animal before.

Riders compete within their division for the following points:

| | |
|---|---|
| 1st  place | 7 points |
| 2nd place | 5 points |
| 3rd place | 4 points |
| 4th place | 3 points |
| 5th place | 2 points |
| 6th place | 1 point |

When more than one rider from the same barn competes in a division, the trainer designates one as the "point rider" before the start of the show. After the judging, only that rider's points count toward the team total.

Areas of the country are divided into zones. For example, Zone 5 consists of Ohio, Kentucky, Indiana, Illinois, and Michigan. Some zones encompass such a large number of teams, as is the case in Zone 5, that they are further divided into regions within the zone.

At the end of the season, around February or March, qualifying teams in each region compete at "Regionals" to determine which will represent the region at the zone level competition, or "Zones." The top four high school teams and the top three middle school teams move on to Zones. The top four high school riders and the top three middle school riders in each class qualify to compete individually at Zones.

The top four teams and individuals in each zone go on to compete at the national level or "Nationals." The location for Nationals changes every year and can be anywhere in the United States.

### *IEA Individual Competition*
Individual riders keep their points whether they were the delegated point rider for the team or not. Individual riders who have accumulated 15 points by the end of the season at the regional level are invited to compete at the zone level and may ultimately go on to compete at the national level as well.

### Horse Names Versus Show Names
Horse owners are permitted to change their horses' names for a competition. This can be great fun for riders and owners and a non-event if you did not know the horse to begin with. However, be forewarned because if you just learned that the big black horse at the barn is named Oreo and then you hear it called Milk's Favorite Cookie, it might be disconcerting.

Usually the show name is a play on the "barn name," for example, Calvin becomes Lord Calvin for shows. Copper becomes Countin' Pennies. Sweetie becomes Sweet Clementine. Oliver becomes Pick Pocket. Some of the names are very clever, so you will want to listen closely as they are announced during the competition.

# 10. Understanding Competitive Divisions and Classes

Going to a show can be even more bewildering than the routine at the barn. You need a basic understanding of the various competitive categories in order to follow the activity at a show and your rider's progress over time.

All shows are organized by divisions which represent the various levels of competition based on ability and age of the rider, and sometimes the experience and size of the horse. The divisions used by OHJA and IEA can be found later in this section and are representative of the categories you will see. Riders in each division compete in different events called classes. The divisions can vary depending on whether it is an IEA, OHJA, or private event, but the actual classes are the same from show to show.

Classes are either "On the Flat" or "Over Fences." Typical classes include:

**Flat class:** There is no jumping involved in this class. Riders are asked to walk, trot and canter their horses according to instructions called out by the judge. In this type of class, all of the riders registered for the class compete in the ring together (unlike the jumping classes in which riders compete one by one).

**Poles:** A long pole is placed on the ground and the rider guides the horse over the pole at a trot. This is the precursor to jumping.

**Crossrails:** Two poles are crossed forming an "X" with the lowest point about 12 inches off the ground. This is the lowest form of a jump that the rider approaches at either a trot or a canter.

**Eighteen Inch:** The measurement refers to the height of the fences that the horse and rider have to negotiate. They can range from 18" to 6' (with the fences being adjusted in six inch increments). Fences top off at 3' 6" for equitation and hunter competitions. Jumpers typically go up to 4' 6"and beyond.

# 11. Show Packing List

## Clothing to wear to the show

- ☐ Shirt (to be worn while you prep the horse so that your show shirt does not get dirty)
- ☐ Riding pants
- ☐ Tall boot socks
- ☐ Paddock boots
- ☐ Team jacket or logo wear from your barn
- ☐ _____
- ☐ _____

## Clothing to wear during the competition

- ☐ Helmet
- ☐ Jacket (in a garment bag)
- ☐ Riding shirt with detachable collar
- ☐ Tall boots (or jodhpurs with garters and boot straps if rider is under nine years old)
- ☐ Gloves
- ☐ Belt
- ☐ Rubber bands
- ☐ Bobby pins
- ☐ Hair ribbons if rider is under nine and wearing braids
  (Note to dads: Don't despair if you are on your own with your daughter. Show moms are generally willing to lend a hand with braids and bows.)
- ☐ Hairnet
- ☐ Small pearl earrings or other tailored earrings are the only acceptable jewelry
- ☐ _____
- ☐ _____

## Equipment

- ☐ Saddle
- ☐ Saddle pad
- ☐ Girth
- ☐ Bridle
- ☐ Martingale
- ☐ Crop
- ☐ Lead rope
- ☐ Small sponge for cleaning tack
- ☐ _____
- ☐ _____

## Show bag or box containing

- ☐ Boot rag
- ☐ Boot polish
- ☐ Hoof polish
- ☐ Hoof pick
- ☐ Water bottle
- ☐ Horse treats
- ☐ Brush
- ☐ Comb for tail and mane
- ☐ Horse fly spray
- ☐ Snacks
- ☐ Activities for down time at the show (homework, I-pod, books, cards)
- ☐ _____
- ☐ _____
- ☐ _____
- ☐ _____

## Horse bath supplies

- ☐ Sponge for bathing horse
- ☐ Squeegee (to remove water from the horse's coat after a bath)
- ☐ Shampoo
- ☐ Rag
- ☐ _____
- ☐ _____

## Additional items

- ☐ Camera
- ☐ Folding chairs
- ☐ Blanket
- ☐ Snacks (most, but not all, shows have a concession stand of some sort)
- ☐ For sunny days:  hat, sunglasses, sunscreen
- ☐ For cold days: extra jacket, warm socks, extra gloves, hats, hand and foot warmers
- ☐ Cash (for concession stands that do not accept credit cards)
- ☐ _____
- ☐ _____
- ☐ _____
- ☐ _____
- ☐ _____
- ☐ _____
- ☐ _____
- ☐ _____

# 12. Show Day Routine

## The day before the show

▶ Bathe and brush the horse.

▶ Pull the mane if too long.

▶ Trim whiskers.

## The morning of the show

▶ Brush the horse's tail and mane.

▶ Brush the horse's coat until it shines.

▶ Lunge the horse if it is too excited so that it will be calm and behave during the class. The trainer, owner, or an experienced rider will lunge the horse for you.

▶ School the horse during a warm up and practice ride.

▶ Apply fly spray during the summer months.

▶ Pick up the rider's number that she will wear around her waist or attach to the horse's bridle during the competition. A rider may not enter the ring without a number.

▶ Pick up a program listing the day's events. You will see that there are no times listed next to the various classes because no one can say in advance how long the classes will take. The more riders sign up for a particular class, the longer it will take for all of them to show. Some shows schedule the youngest riders first, others begin with the more experienced riders, and yet others have both groups competing simultaneously in two separate rings. Your trainer will give you an idea as to when your rider might compete.

## During the show

▶ Until you are experienced at interpreting a jumping course diagram, allow the trainer to help the rider memorize the course, i.e., which direction she is supposed to go in the ring and in which order to go over the jumps. The trainer will also review how many strides the horse or pony is to take between the jumps.

❯ Do not talk to a rider in the ring. Leave the instructive comments to the trainer.

❯ Clap for riders when they finish a class or as they leave the ring. Do not applaud if the rider has been disqualified by falling off, having the horse refuse to go over a jump three times, or going off course.

❯ Be ready to help your rider. She will need a lot of assistance at the show to get herself and her horse ready. Once the rider is on the horse, she is bound to need something, such as a drink of water, a crop, or a rag to polish her boots just before going into the ring.

**After the show**

❯ Untack the horse.

❯ Bathe the horse.

❯ Feed the horse.

❯ Give the horse treats for a job well done.

# 13. Judging Basics

The following are some of the skills the judge will want to see the rider demonstrate during competition.

**Diagonal while trotting:**
You will see that the rider is posting, going up and down in the saddle, during a trot. The judge will be checking to see if the rider is up, out of the saddle, when the horse's outside leg is extended in front. The judge can easily detect the correct rhythm but you may want to remember this little saying, "Rise and fall with the leg on the wall."

**Lead while cantering:**
When you watch a horse canter, you will see that the step has a three beat rhythm to it. The judge will be watching to see if the horse's inside front leg is always taking the first of those three beats. Getting on the wrong lead is a serious offense. The rider must correct it immediately or risk not even placing in the class.

**Strides when jumping:**
When two fences are set up one after the other in a straight line, they are carefully spaced so that a horse will take a certain number of steps, or strides, between them. The number of strides permitted is noted on the course diagram. A pony will naturally have a shorter stride than a horse and would be expected to take seven or eight strides while a horse would take five or six. If a horse takes fewer strides, it is going too fast; too many strides mean the horse is going too slowly. The judge will be watching to see that the rider paces the horse so that it takes the appropriate number of strides between fences.

The judge also looks for specific abilities according to the type of classes being judged: equitation, hunter or jumper.

**EQUITATION:**
In an equitation class, the judges score the riders on a point system. They are watching for a myriad of details that are not readily apparent to anyone new to the sport. The judge will be looking for the rider's overall presentation, including proper attire. Points are taken away for flashy earrings, socks showing above the boots, and clothing stained with horse slobber. They will note details in technique such as the rider's posture (shoulders back), position of the hands, legs (perfectly still) and

feet (heels pointing toward the ground).  The judge will also evaluate the rider's ability to control the horse.  The judge will not take into consideration the breed, color, or build of the horse in an equitation class.

*Crossrails Equitation:*
The judge will be watching to see if the rider maintains an even pace, if the horse approaches the crossrails straight on rather than at an angle, and if the horse jumps in the center where the two poles cross.  The judge will also count the strides between jumps that are set up in a straight line.

*Equitation Over Fences:*
In these classes, horse and rider navigate a series of fences in the ring.  The judge is looking for the rider's form and ability to control the horse.  Points are deducted if a horse refuses to go over a jump, knocks down a fence, or throws its rider. After three refusals or being thrown, a rider is disqualified.

## HUNTER:
In a hunter class, the horse is being judged rather than the rider. The judge observes the build of the horse, how it moves, its temperament, and its form when jumping.  In addition, the judge will be watching for the leads and strides discussed above.

*Under Saddle:*
This is another name for a flat class in which the judge is grading the horse rather than the rider.  A trainer will take a "green" horse to a show and compete in an under saddle class to accustom it to being in the ring with other horses.

## JUMPER:
Horse and rider navigate a series of fences in the ring as in the hunter class.  However, the judge is not looking at the horse's form, but rather its speed.  The objective is to finish the course in the least amount of time without knocking any of the fences down.

## OPEN DIVISIONS:
Most horse shows offer open divisions in which trainers and professional riders can practice with young horses before they are shown by young riders in an amateur division.  These classes are judged on the horse and are sometimes used as warm-up classes.

## PRIZES

Ribbons are awarded to the top six or seven riders in each class. At some shows, the riders with the most accumulated points in a division are awarded Champion (top honor) and Reserve Champion (runner up). A form is included at the end of this guide for you to use to track your rider's progress at shows.

### INDIVIDUAL CLASS PRIZE:

| Ribbon Color | Significance |
| --- | --- |
| Blue | First Place |
| Red | Second Place |
| Yellow | Third Place |
| White | Fourth Place |
| Pink | Fifth Place |
| Green | Sixth Place |

### OVERALL DIVISION PRIZE:

| Tri-color Ribbon | Significance |
| --- | --- |
| Blue, red, yellow | Champion |
| Red, yellow, white | Reserve Champion |

Of course, everyone wishes for a first place, but in horseback riding, placing at all is a significant accomplishment. Sixth place is a success for the rider competing in a class of 15 riders. It is also an important win for a rider who has not placed at all in that particular class before.

# 14. The Cost Of Showing

There are two components to the cost of a horse show, namely, the amount charged by your barn and trainer and the amount charged by the show's organizers. How much you owe depends in large part on whether you take "your" horse to the show the morning of the show itself or the night before. There are pros and cons to both options.

| | ADVANTAGES | DISADVANTAGES |
|---|---|---|
| **Bringing the horse the day of the show** | ❯ There is no boarding fee.<br><br>❯ The horse is under your supervision at all times. | ❯ You will have to get up at the crack of dawn to drive to the barn, get the horse into the trailer, and drive to the show.<br><br>❯ The horse is unaccustomed to the surroundings, sounds, and other horses. The horse may be tired or stressed and not perform well. |
| **Bringing the horse the night before the show** | ❯ The horse will be more relaxed and acclimated.<br><br>❯ You still have to get up early, but not as early as the people who are trailering their horses that morning. | ❯ There will be extra boarding costs.<br><br>❯ You may not feel comfortable leaving your horse at an unfamiliar barn overnight. |

**Expenses incurred at your barn:**

◗ Hauling – Taking the horse to the show in a special horse trailer. Your trainer can help with these arrangements if you will be using someone else's horse.

◗ Grooming

◗ Schooling – A short class with your trainer the morning of the show to get the horse warmed up and in the right frame of mind.

◗ Training Fee – Compensation for the time the trainer spends prepping the rider for classes each day.

◗ Usage Fee -- Use of the horse if it is not covered under a leasing agreement.

**Plus... Expenses incurred at the show:**

◗ Horse stall

◗ Bedding for the stall

◗ Schooling – Use of a ring to practice with the horse before the show starts.

◗ Price per class – There is a fee charged per class which varies according to the prestige of the show. The trainer will decide in what division and classes the rider will compete. When showing individually, a rider would typically compete in three to five classes. When showing as a team, each member typically shows in only one or two classes.

# 15. Ohio Hunter Jumper Divisions

Below are simplified descriptions of the OHJA divisions. Just remember, the higher the fence, the more experienced the rider must be.

## Equitation:

| DIVISION NAME | AGE LIMIT | FENCE HEIGHT |
|---|---|---|
| Walk/Trot Equitation | Divided between ≤8 and 9+ | Poles |
| Crossrails Equitation | Divided between ≤9 and 10+ | Crossrails |
| 11 and Under Equitation | | 2' to 2' 6" |
| Short Stirrup Equitation | 11 years or younger | 1' 6" to 2' 3" |
| Limit Rider Equitation | 12 years and up | 1' 6" |
| Intermediate Children's Equitation | | 2' 6" |
| 12-14 Equitation | | 3' |
| 15-17 Equitation | | 3' to 3' 6" |
| Adult Equitation | 18 years and up | 3' to 3' 6" |
| Intermediate Adult Equitation | 18 years and up | 2' 6" |

## Hunter:

| DIVISION NAME | AGE LIMIT | FENCE HEIGHT |
|---|---|---|
| Short Stirrup Hunter | 11 years or less | 1' 6" to 2' 3" |
| Special Hunter | | 2' 6" |
| Intermediate Children's Hunter | Junior Exhibitor | 2' 6" |
| Medium Pony Hunter | | 2' 6" |
| Small Pony Hunter | | 2' 6" |
| Limit Rider Hunter | 12 years and up | 1' 6" to 2' 3" |
| Large Pony Hunter | | 3' |
| Junior Hunter | Junior Exhibitor | 3' 3" to 3' 6" |
| Amateur/Owner Hunter | 18 years or older | 3' 3" to 3' 6" |
| Pre-Green Hunter | | 2' 9" to 3' 6" |
| Open Working Hunter | | 3' 3" to 3' 6" |
| Low Hunter | | 3' |
| Children's Hunter | Junior Exhibitor | 2' 9" to 3' 3" |
| Adult Amateur Hunter | 18 years or older | 2' 9" to 3' 3" |
| Intermediate Adult Hunter | 18 years or older | 2' 6" |
| Children's Pony Hunter | Junior Exhibitor | 2' or 2' 6" |
| Green Hunter | | 3' 3" to 3' 9" |

## Jumper:

| DIVISION NAME | AGE LIMIT | FENCE HEIGHT |
|---|---|---|
| Schooling/Training Jumper | | 3' to 3' 6" |
| Children's/Adult Jumper | | 3' to 3' 6" |
| Intermediate Children's/Adult Jumper | | 2' 6" to 2' 9" |

# 16. Interscholastic Equestrian Association Divisions

Interscholastic Equestrian Association (IEA) is open to students beginning in 6th through 12th grade. Riders are divided between middle school and high school teams. The middle school teams are referred to as "Futures." The high school riders are either on the Junior Varsity or Varsity teams.

| DIVISION NUMBER* | DIVISION NAME | FENCE HEIGHT |
|---|---|---|
| 2 | Varsity Open Equitation Over Fences | 2' 6" |
| 3 | Varsity Intermediate Equitation Over Fences | 2' |
| 4 | Junior Varsity Novice Equitation Over Fences | Crossrails |
| 5 | Future Intermediate Equitation Over Fences | 2' |
| 6 | Future Novice Over Fences | Crossrails |
| 8 | Varsity Open Equitation on the Flat | n/a |
| 9 | Varsity Intermediate Equitation on the Flat | n/a |
| 10 | JV Novice Equitation on the Flat | n/a |
| 11 | JV Beginner Equitation on the Flat | n/a |
| 12 | Future Intermediate Equitation on the Flat | n/a |
| 13 | Future Novice Equitation on the Flat | n/a |

*Here is one of those enigmas of the sport – there are no Divisions 1 or 7. Go figure.*

# 17. College Teams and Scholarships

In case you are hoping that eventually you might recoup some of the expense incurred for horseback riding lessons and shows in the form of a college scholarship, you may be disappointed.

The National Collegiate Athletic Association (NCAA) considers horseback riding an "emerging sport." That means that some schools consider horseback riding an NCAA sport but not the 40 schools required to sanction an NCAA National Championship. As of 2007, 24 schools in the country met the criteria.

Maybe by the time **your** daughter is in college it will be an official NCAA sport and scholarships will abound. For the time being, however, horseback riding is usually considered a club sport. Many colleges and universities have competitive equestrian teams that follow rules similar to IEA.

# COMPETITION TRACKER

SHOW:

DATE:

DIVISION:

| CLASS NUMBER | CLASS DESCRIPTION | PLACE | NUMBER OF COMPETITORS |
|---|---|---|---|
| 1 | | | |
| 2 | | | |
| 3 | | | |
| 4 | | | |
| 5 | | | |
| | | | |
| | | | |

☐ Champion

☐ Reserve Champion

# 18. Resources

## ASSOCIATIONS FOR COMPETITIVE RIDING

❯ Ohio Hunter/Jumper Association:  www.OHJA.net

❯ Interscholastic Equestrian Association:  www.rideiea.com/

❯ Tri-state Horse Show Association:  www.tristatehs.com/

❯ Intercollegiate Horse Show Association (college level competition):  http://www.ihsainc.com/

## HORSEBACK RIDING EVENTS WHERE YOU CAN SEE PROFESSIONAL RIDERS COMPETE

❯ Rolex Three-Day Event, The Kentucky Horsepark, Lexington, Kentucky (April):  http://www.rk3de.org/

The three-day event starts with dressage in an arena on Friday, so children miss a day of school to attend.  Spectators are seated on bleachers to watch and are expected to maintain silence while the horses and riders are in the ring. Smaller children will be bored watching dressage which is all about details and control.

Day two is the cross country competition.  This takes place in acres of open field.  Spectators can choose to walk from fence to fence or stay near a particularly interesting jump to see how each of the horses navigates over it.  Cross country is very exciting to watch, but it is an extreme sport and every year there are one or two riders and horses hurt and taken away in ambulances.

Day three the riders and their horses jump fences in a stadium.  This is a more formal event than the cross country race so the riders wear their formal riding attire and there are fewer dramatic accidents.

Throughout the weekend there are booths selling every imaginable item related to horses from jewelry to shoe inserts.  It is fascinating to wander through the aisles learning how serious horse people spend their money.  There are also special times throughout the day during which the competitors are available for photos and autographs.

◗The New Albany Classic, Columbus, Ohio (September): http://www.thenewalbanyclassic.com/

◗Equine Affaire, Ohio State fairgrounds (April): http://www.equineaffaire.com/ohio/

◗The World Equestrian Games, Kentucky Horse Park (September-October, 2010): http://www.feigames2010.org/

◗Equitana, An international equine event which alternates between the U.S. and Europe  http://www.equitana.com/

◗The FEI World Cup.  Competition on a global scale: www.feiworldcup.org


## BOOKS FOR THE HORSE LOVER

### Grade School:

*The Saddle Club* – A series that tracks the adventures of a group of girls who ride at the same barn.

*The Black Stallion* – This famous book by Walter Farley spawned a series.

*Heartland* – A series by Lauren Brooke about a girl who works with rescue horses.

*Chestnut Hill* – A series by Lauren Brooke about girls who live together at a boarding school and love horses.

*Misty of Chincoteague* -- This book written by Marguerite Henry, is based on a true story of a filly born to a wild horse. There are several sequels.

### High School:

*Chicken Soup for the Horse Lover's Soul I and II* – Short, inspirational stories by a variety of authors.

*Horse Miracles: Inspirational True Stories of Remarkable Horses* – Brad Steigert and Sherry Hansen Steigert

*Chosen by a Horse* – Written by Susan Richards.

## A MAGAZINE SUBSCRIPTION APPROPRIATE FOR NEW RIDERS

*Young Rider*

 NOTES

 NOTES

 NOTES

 NOTES

#  NOTES

 # NOTES